natural
SOAP MAKING

natural SOAP MAKING

Elizabeth Letcavage, editor

Melissa Harden, expert consultant

photographs by Alan Wycheck

STACKPOLE
BOOKS

Published by
STACKPOLE BOOKS
5067 Ritter Road
Mechanicsburg, PA 17055
www.stackpolebooks.com

Printed in the United States of America

10 9 8 7 6 5 4 3 2 1

First edition

Cover design by Wendy A. Reynolds

Library of Congress Cataloging-in-Publication Data

Natural soap making / Elizabeth Letcavage, editor ; Melissa Harden, expert consultant ; photographs by Alan Wycheck. — First edition.
      pages cm
   ISBN 978-0-8117-1072-5
   1. Soap. I. Letcavage, Elizabeth, editor.
   TP991.N28 2013
   668'.12—dc23
                                   2012034474

Contents

Foreword

Soap making can be a wonderfully rewarding scientific experiment or a practical hobby producing special handmade products for personal or professional use—or both at the same time.

With my master's degree in engineering, I was especially intrigued by the scientific, chemical nature of cold process soap making. I've also always loved to bake, and I found that developing scientifically derived recipes for handmade soaps fed both my loves. I loved experimenting with various oil and butter combinations, developing different fragrance patterns, and using natural colorants, additives, textures, soap shapes, and multi-soap combinations.

I was amazed at how long my handmade soap lasted and that it could be used for both skin and hair. I sincerely hope you enjoy making cold process soap as much as I do and allow yourself to expand your mind creatively. There are no boundaries to what you can do with soap.

Melissa Harden

Introduction

The wonderful properties of natural handmade soap amaze and thrill beginners and veterans alike. Once you learn the process of making soap using the recipes in this book, you may find that you will be creatively driven to experiment with other ingredients. There are hundreds of possible combinations of oils and butters, fragrances, and botanical additives that make each bar unique. The different ingredients you can use in handmade soaps fulfill specific purposes, such as moisturizing, exfoliating, taming oily skin, or simply cleaning.

In the past, people made their own soap out of necessity. Today, inexpensive, mass-produced soap may be found on the shelves of every grocery store and pharmacy. But you can still easily transform natural ingredients into luxurious skin-care bars that are incomparable to the factory-made ones.

This book's step-by-step instructions and detailed photographs will enable you to experience the rewards of making your own soaps for hands, face, and body.

Expect some happy surprises and some disappointments as you experiment with different combinations of ingredients. Soap making is part science, part art. Making notes on what worked and what didn't will improve your skills and knowledge and result in many more hits than misses.

Chances are that once you make your own soap, you'll never go back to store bought. Enjoy!

Chapter 1

Equipment & Ingredients

Making soap "batter" is a fast process, so you'll want to have your workspace prepared and all of your ingredients, equipment, and supplies at the ready.

The most convenient workspace is a kitchen; however, soap may be made elsewhere. You should make sure you have a sturdy table and access to electricity if you opt to use electric-powered tools instead of hand-powered ones.

Read on, assemble your supplies, and get ready to have some fun!

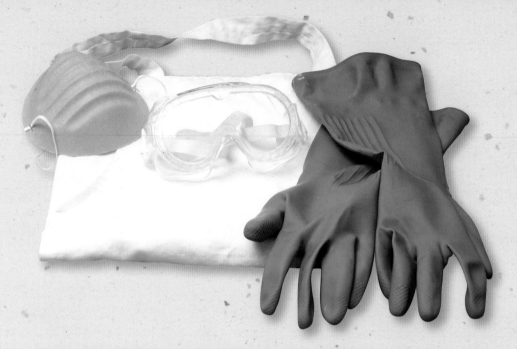

Most of the equipment and supplies you'll need can be found in an ordinary kitchen. The one major exception is a digital scale. This is one tool that is essential, as a successful soap recipe requires that all of the major ingredients—sodium hydroxide (lye), water, oils, and butters—be measured precisely by weight. If the lye and water mixture is too strong, the resulting soap could be too harsh and burn the skin. If it is too weak, the resulting soap will be a mushy mess that will disintegrate quickly when used.

Select a scale that measures weight in tenth-ounce increments and has a tare (reset to zero) feature. Scales are available that run on AC current, batteries, or either power source.

SAFE SOAP MAKING

Sodium hydroxide (lye) is the one ingredient in soap making that is dangerous; it is extremely caustic and must be handled with great care. Gloves, eye protection, a dust mask, and an apron should be used when mixing the water and lye. Gloves and an apron should be worn throughout the mixing process. No protection is needed for unmolding and cutting the soap, as the soap will be fully saponified at that point.

Because of the hazards of using lye, cold process soap making is not recommended as an activity for children.

Working with Sodium Hydroxide

- Keep lye away from skin, eyes, mouth, and clothing.
- Do not handle lye in the presence of children or animals.
- Keep lye in a dry, sealed, nonmetallic container.
- Keep lye in a locked or secure area.
- Always mix lye and water in a well-ventilated area.
- Always wear protective clothing when handling lye.
- Do not use aluminum pots or utensils with lye, as they chemically react with one another.

THE "SOAP COOK'S" POTS, BOWLS, AND UTENSILS

Sodium hydroxide reacts adversely with aluminum, so your bowls, stirrers, utensils, and molds must be made of plastic, silicone, or non-aluminum metals such as stainless steel.

Before you begin mixing your ingredients, have the following tools ready to go:

Measuring Cups and Containers

You'll need containers that are large enough to hold the quantity of each oil and butter called for in your recipe. Because these liquid ingredients are measured by weight, you don't need calibrated cups, but clear, heat-resistant, glass measuring cups work well. You can also use plastic food storage containers.

There are some soap additives, however, that are measured by volume. You'll need a set of measuring spoons and cups to calculate amounts of fragrance, essential oils, and botanical additives such as oats, herbs, flowers, and leaves.

Stirrers

Soap is made by combining a sodium hydroxide/water mixture with various oils and butters. The easiest and fastest way to do this is with an electric stick blender, a tool that is well worth the investment. If you don't have an electric stick blender, you can use your favorite rubber or silicone spoon or spatula. Don't use utensils made of aluminum, tin, iron, or Teflon. Wood should also be avoided as it tends to disintegrate and splinter.

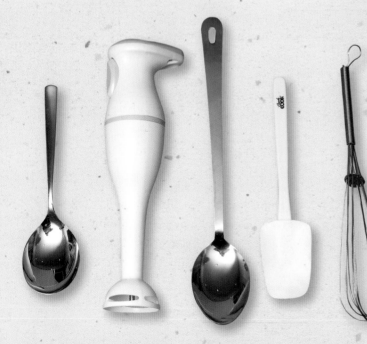

Thermometer

When sodium hydroxide and water are combined, the mixture becomes very hot. A candy thermometer is used to determine when the mixture has cooled enough to add to the oils and butters.

Cutting Tools

A sturdy chef's knife or a pastry cutter can be used to cut soap bricks into bars. A cutter with a serrated blade will add an interesting texture to finished soaps. Those planning to make lots of soap or start a business will want to invest in a special soap cutter designed specifically to slice bars evenly and to a consistent size.

Mortar and Pestle or Coffee Grinder

Some soap additives must be crushed or ground prior before they're added to the soap mixture. A mortar and pestle provides more control over the size of the finished product, but an electric coffee grinder is speedier.

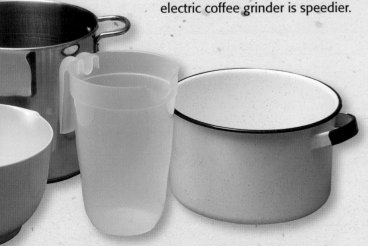

Pots and Pitchers

Select a non-aluminum pot or bowl large enough to hold the combined total of all the ingredients in your soap recipe. Stainless steel or enamel-coated pots are the best choices. Avoid pots made of tin, iron, Teflon, and cast iron. In the step-by-step process that follows, the plastic pitcher is used to mix the sodium hydroxide and water.

ADDITIONAL ITEMS

Counter or Table Covering

Newspapers, old bed sheets, or dollar-store plastic tablecloths may be used to protect your countertop or table.

Bath and Beach Towels

Have plenty of towels on hand to place under and over your soap molds to keep them warm as they cure.

Vegetable Peeler

A standard kitchen vegetable peeler can be used to tidy up soap bar edges.

Mold Lining Material

Freezer paper or parchment paper may be used to line soap molds. The dull side is placed against the sides of the mold; the waxy or glossy side prevents the soap from sticking.

Distilled Water

Because of the potential impurities in rainwater and chemicals in tap water, distilled water is preferred for soap making. However, any drinkable water may be used to make your soap.

Cutting Board

A wood or plastic cutting board protects your work surface when cutting soap bricks into bars.

Drying Surface

Once soaps are cut they are allowed to dry on waxed paper, parchment paper, plastic needlework canvas, or plastic window screening.

Clear Plastic Wrap

Have a roll of plastic wrap on hand to cover the surface of the soap mixture in the mold.

Soap Molds

Finished soap "batter" is poured into molds, wrapped in towels to keep warm, and "put to bed" to cure. Soap making has become so popular that many craft stores and online sellers offer ready-made wood, plastic, acrylic, and silicon soap molds.

Wood Molds

These will keep the soap warmer during the curing process than plastic will and can endure years of hard use, but they must be lined with parchment paper or freezer paper to prevent the soap from sticking. The long, deep wood soap mold shown here and used in the following instructions makes a 4- to 5-pound soap brick. The interior measures $12\frac{3}{4}$ by $3\frac{1}{4}$ by $3\frac{1}{4}$ inches. The soap mold tray shown measures 9 by 12 by $1\frac{3}{4}$ inches and is used in the directions for making cutout soaps. About 2 pounds of soap will make a slab $\frac{1}{2}$ inch thick in a mold this size, while 3 pounds of soap will make a slab $\frac{3}{4}$ inch thick. Purchased molds will come with a lid. A piece of scrap wood or heavy cardboard can also be used to top the mold. The goal is to retain the heat, so the lid need not be tight fitting and it may extend over the top edges of the mold.

Acrylic, Plastic, and Silicone Molds

Soap molds in fanciful shapes and unique designs abound. Great as party favors or gifts, shaped soaps are a fun alternative to the standard bar. Molds designed for use in candy or cupcake making may be also be used instead of soap molds. Beginner soap makers should consider mastering making bricks before taking on these molded soaps; you have to work quickly to pour the soap before it sets up and becomes too thick to work with. Molds are widely available at craft and cooking stores and through online sellers.

Plastic Food Storage Containers

Heavy-duty plastic containers with snap-on lids also may be used to make soap. Because they are pliable, they do not need to be lined; however, a liner will make the unmolding process easier and faster. Keep in mind that the soap will conform to curved corners, and any indentations in the container will be molded into the soap.

Sodium Hydroxide (Lye)

The chemical reaction of the sodium hydroxide with water and fat is what creates cold process soap. Lye can be difficult to find in small quantities at retail stores, but some hardware and grocery stores carry it as a drain cleaner. Only select a product that is labeled "100% sodium hydroxide."

Oils

A variety of liquid oils are available at grocery and discount stores. Inexpensive oils will produce the same results as pricier oils. This is especially true with olive oil. Virgin or extra virgin oils produce less foam and dissolve too quickly; instead, select oil from the first pressing or the one that is the lightest in color.

Solid oils need to be melted prior to adding them to the water/sodium hydroxide solution. Palm and coconut are popular soap making oils which are solid at room temperature. You can even use everyday cooking shortening to make an inexpensive bar of soap. Check the label to find out the specific blend of oils used in a particular brand.

Butters

Butters are the fats pressed from the kernels of plants and are solid at room temperature. Health food stores, pharmacies, and online vendors are good sources for butters. Butters are melted prior to adding to the water/sodium hydroxide solution.

Cocoa, hemp seed, shea, and mango butters are rich skin conditioners and will contribute to a hard bar. Cocoa butter is the only one that will add fragrance to handmade soap.

PROPERTIES AND BENEFITS OF POPULAR OILS AND BUTTERS

Oils are selected for the specific properties they impart to the soap: soft and fast dissolving or hard and longer lasting; fluffy, stable lather or little lather; mildness or harshness; cleansing or moisturizing. Some oils contain antioxidants and vitamins. Some are inexpensive and some costly. Below are the features and benefits of just some of the oils available to the soapmaker. By experimenting with different combinations, you will find the right recipe for the results you seek.

Avocado Oil

Because it is easily absorbed into deep tissue and has wonderful emollient properties, avocado oil is ideal for mature skin. This oil is high in sterolins (which are reputed to help soften the skin and impart a superior moisturizing effect) and assists in the regeneration and rejuvenation of the skin. This oil contributes to a soft bar of soap with a foamy, stable lather. It's a good oil to use to "superfat" soap recipes (see page 22). It makes soap extra rich and creamy.

Castor Oil

Castor oil acts as a humectant (draws moisture from the air) and an emollient (softens and smooths) for the skin. It helps make a hard bar of soap with lots of lather and is especially well suited for shampoo bars and skin-care products. Note that the more castor oil used in a recipe, the softer the soap will be.

Coconut Oil

This is one of the main soap making base oils. This oil makes a hard bar with lots of lather for deep cleansing. It has a longer shelf life than most oils. Use this oil in combination with other moisturizing oils (you can use coconut oil for up to 25 percent of the total oil) to counter coconut oil's drying effect.

Grapeseed Oil

This oil is a rich source of linoleic acid, which results in a mild soap that conditions the skin. It's a great lubricant and an ideal carrier oil for use in body scrubs. This odorless oil has a shorter shelf life than other oils. It can be found at most well-stocked grocery stores, but it is fairly expensive so is used sparingly.

Choosing Oils

Some oils are selected for specific properties they will impart to the soap:

Skin Conditioners: Almond, canola, castor, corn, hazelnut, hemp seed, jojoba, olive, peanut, safflower, sesame, soybean, and sunflower oils.

Firm or Hard Bar: Coconut, lanolin, palm kernel, palm, and rice bran oils.

Shea, mango, and hemp seed butters (from left to right) are solid at room temperature and must be melted prior to use.

Sweet Almond Oil

This oil is an excellent emollient and helps the skin to absorb and retain moisture. It is a light, non-greasy, penetrating oil that is excellent for all skin types. It makes a stable lather and helps condition the skin.

Olive Oil

This is one of the main soap making base oils, popular for its moisturizing properties and its ability to attract external moisture to the skin and form a breathable layer to prevent the loss of internal moisture. It will not block the natural functions of the skin. Soap made with 100 percent olive oil is referred to as "Castile soap." It produces a very mild, soft soap.

Palm Oil

This is one oil that is used in conjunction with other oils when you want to produce a hard bar of soap that will hold up during use. It produces a creamy, stable lather. It makes a mild bar that cleanses well. Also known as "vegetable tallow," it is a higher quality oil than vegetable oils.

Jojoba Oil

This is one of the most expensive oils, but one of the best to enhance your skin's natural oils. This oil is the most like the natural oil our own skin produces and works in harmony with our skin to replenish and protect. Jojoba oil helps unclog pores and has deep cleansing properties. It has a long shelf life and produces a soft bar.

Cocoa Butter

This butter lays down a protective layer that holds moisture to the skin. It works extremely well with other luxurious oils like olive, jojoba, castor, or avocado, which help it become absorbed into the skin. This butter will produce a hard bar that will remain stable much longer than most soaps. It leaves skin feeling very soft and silky. Natural cocoa butter has a "chocolately" scent that will be imparted in your final bar. Make sure to pair a scent that goes well with a chocolate scent.

Shea Butter

This is an unscented butter that is also great to use with skin lotions. Shea butter can also be used directly as a moisturizer. It has a high percentage of unsaponifables, which means that a high portion of the shea butter used in a recipe does not react with the lye to form soap. It is left in its original state within the bar, leaving it able to moisturize and nourish the skin. It is purported to protect skin from the harmful effects of the sun and help heal scars.

Mango Butter

This butter is one of the most highly prized oils in bath products. Like shea butter, it has a high percentage of unsaponifables, so that a large percentage of its original state is left within the bar, leaving it able to moisturize and nourish the skin. It's used to protect skin from harmful effects of the sun and heal damaged skin. It's a good oil to use to "superfat" soap.

ADDITIVES TRANSFORM SOAP FROM BASIC TO BEAUTIFUL

The combination of oils you select will determine the degree of lather, bar hardness, and skin conditioning properties of the soap. Other natural additives impart unique textures, colors, and fragrances to homemade soap. It is through additives that you can produce a soap that stimulates the senses.

Flecks of loose tea serve as a mild exfoliant in this soap.

A few good exfoliating additives are shown here. Surrounding the center bowl of cornmeal, counterclockwise from front, are: oats, white pumice (fine sand), ground vanilla bean, cinnamon, blackberry seeds, and apricot seeds.

Botanicals for Texture and Skin Conditioning

Herbs, spices, flowers, leaves, beans, seeds, clays, and charcoal are used in soap to add texture and visual interest. Through these additives, you can create a mild exfoliating soap that will brighten facial skin by removing a light layer of dead skin cells, or an extreme cleansing bar that can rid gardener's hands of soil or a mechanic's hands of grease and grime.

The effectiveness of the bar is controlled by which additives you choose and how coarsely they are ground. An electric coffee grinder or a mortar and pestle are used to prepare ingredients to the desired fineness. Seeds, pumice, and charcoal, and slightly ground oatmeal are the best texture additives for hand and body soaps. Finely ground oats, cornmeal, and sea clays are wonderful additions to facial bars.

Exfoliants

Cinnamon
Use this common spice right out of your kitchen stock or save by purchasing it in bulk at health food stores or soap supply sellers.

Cornmeal
This natural additive can be found at the grocery store.

Lavender
In addition to finding food- or cosmetic-grade lavender at soap supply stores, it is almost always sold by shops that sell herbs and potpourri making supplies, as it has a healthy, aromatherapeutic scent.

Lemongrass
Often used in Asian food, this grass may be found dried and ground in health and Asian food stores and through soap making suppliers.

Loose Tea
You can use your favorite loose-leaf tea or open up a teabag.

Pumice (Fine Sand)
Pumice, formed from volcanic rock lava, is finely ground for use in soap as an exfoliant. It is available from online soap making supply vendors.

Oats
Another additive that comes from the grocery store shelf, oats are a common ingredient to add scrubability to soap. Select rolled oats or traditional oatmeal flakes, not the instant type.

Seeds
Apricot, blackberry, poppy, and several other fruit seeds add exfoliating power to hand and body bars. They are available at health food stores, through soap making suppliers, and in the grocery store.

Lavender flowers will have a nicer appearance in soap if they are slightly ground.

Poppy seeds (bar on left) and blackberry seeds (bar on right) add exfoliating properties and an interesting texture to handmade soap.

Tapioca Pearls

This starch is extracted from the tropical plant known as the cassava or boba and is used in many food recipes. It's a gentle exfoliant additive that's good for facial bars. Find it in health or Asian food stores or through soap making supply vendors.

Wheat Germ

This food additive is readily available at grocery and health food stores.

> **O**ther additives will help normalize oily skin or moisturize dry skin. You can also add natural ingredients that act as deodorizers, antioxidants, and antibacterial agents.

Conditioners

Aloe Vera Gel

This plant extract hydrates and soothes dry skin and is commonly sold by herbalists and pharmacies.

Beeswax

Beeswax produces a hard bar that lays down a protective layer to moisturize and soften the skin. It is available in small blocks or pellets at health food stores, some gardening shops, and soap making supply vendors. It is malted and mixed with the oils before they are added to the water–sodium hydroxide mixture.

Calendula

This dried flower softens rough skin and is the only flower that will keep its yellow color through the saponification process. Other flowers may be used as exfoliants, but keep in mind that they will turn brown or black during saponification.

Clays

Pink kaolin clay has high iron oxide content, while green sea clay is rich in minerals and algaes. Both remove excess oil toxins and impurities from the skin but should be used in moderation or they will dry out skin too much. Moroccan red clay draws oils from the skin and acts as an astringent.

Milks

Rich in fats and emollients, goat milk, buttermilk, and coconut milk smooth, cleanse, and moisturize skin. Buttermilk makes a luxurious lather. All are available at well-stocked grocery stores.

Use cosmetic-grade beeswax, either in its natural yellow form or bleached (by the sun) as shown here. It is available in bars, bricks, and pellets. Buttermilk enhances the lather of a soap and can easily be found in grocery stores.

A Note on Adding Liquids

When adding liquids, such as goat milk, buttermilk, or coconut milk, decrease the amount of water in the initial lye solution by the quantity of liquid you are adding. For example, if you add 2 ounces of milk to the basic soap recipe, decrease the amount of water by 2 ounces. Use milks immediately after opening. Do not use more than 2 ounces of Vitamin E in a recipe; with more than 2 ounces the saponification values would need to be recalculated.

Medicinals

Beeswax
In addition to serving as a skin conditioner, beeswax purportedly has antibacterial, antiseptic, and wound-healing properties.

Cinnamon
This spice is a natural deodorant.

Coconut Milk
In addition to serving as a skin conditioner, coconut milk has antibacterial and antifungal properties.

Lemon Oil
The oil extracted from lemon rinds helps eliminate bacteria and is a natural deodorant.

Vitamin E
The liquid form serves as an antioxidant. (Do not use more than 2 ounces in the basic recipes provided in this book.) It is widely available at health food stores and pharmacies.

Tea Tree Oil
This oil is extracted from the leaves of an Australian tree. Its antiseptic, antifungal, and antiviral properties make it attractive to herbalists in the treatment of acne, sunburn, infection, athlete's foot, rashes, dandruff, and other minor skin irritations.

Nature provides ingredients for coloring handmade soap. A few commonly used ones are: (clockwise from left) ground vanilla bean, cinnamon, turmeric, paprika, and cocoa.

Colorants

Herbs, spices, flowers, clays, and other natural ingredients will add soft, earthy colors to your soap. Most common are light shades of yellow, orange, green, pink, purple, and brown. Black and dark brown, which are obtained by adding charcoal and cocoa, will make a masculine or sophisticated-looking soap.

The color range for soaps containing natural ingredients is limited, so some soap makers who want stronger, brighter colors will use synthetic colors made from minerals. Natural mineral oxide pigments, mica, and dyes are available from soap making suppliers and online vendors in dozens of colors, including neon brights. These can be tricky to use, however, as some may react with fragrance and essential oils and produce unexpected results. Use only cosmetic- or food-grade colorants and use the quantity specified on the product label.

Charcoal, pink kaolin clay, and green clay do double duty in soap. All are colorants that also remove impurities and help dry oily skin.

Nettle leaf will produce a strong green color and is thought to help relieve itchy skin.

Natural Soap Color Selector

Brown
Cinnamon
Cocoa
Honey

Black
Charcoal (you can get eco-friendly charcoal made from bamboo)
Alkanet Root Powder (if a large amount is used)

Green
French Green Clay
Nettle Leaf

Purple
Alkanet Root Powder (depending on the amount used, the resulting color can range from light purple to dark purple to black)

Yellow
Turmeric

Yellow/Orange
Annatto Seed
Paprika
Turmeric

Peach/Pink
Paprika
Pink Kaolin or Rose Clay

Red
Red Moroccan Clay

Preparing Herbs for Use in Soap

Leaves of herbs such as mint, nettle leaf, and lemon balm are dried before use in soaps. If you wish to use homegrown herbs, select those that are healthy, unblemished, and not chemically treated. Cut the stems early in the morning and rinse briefly under running water. Place the herbs on a screen or tray and leave them in an airy place out of direct sunlight. It will take from a few days to a week for the herbs to dry; the time will depend on the type of herb, temperature, and humidity, so check them periodically. When they are completely dry and crumbly, strip the leaves off the stems and store them in an airtight container. Grind as needed.

Honey
Honey lays down a protective film on the skin that hydrates and soothes it. To avoid having the honey seep out after the bar has solidified, keep the amounts down to about 2 teaspoons for every pound of fats and oils.

A nice range of organic colors can be produced with natural additives. These soaps were colored with (from left) paprika, honey, turmeric, nettle leaf, pink kaolin clay, coffee, and alkanet root.

Depending on how much you use, paprika can produce soap that is light yellow or light orange.

Make Infusions with Botanicals

Another method of adding color to your soap is through the infusion process. To make an infusion, you steep a botanical ingredient (seeds, leaves, or powder) in oil, much as you would use tea leaves to make hot tea. Making your own infusion colorants is another aspect of soap making that requires experimentation and experience to get the desired results. Color additives can actually change color through the saponification process or become lighter or darker than expected.

A common botanical that makes orange when infused is annatto seeds. Measure 2 tablespoons of the oil you will be using in your recipe into a small microwavable bowl. Add 1 tablespoon of annatto seeds. Microwave the mixture for 20 seconds on full power. Remove the bowl and let the mixture cool for a minute, then microwave again for 20 seconds on full power. Allow the mixture to sit until the desired color is reached, then strain out the annatto seeds.

Note that you will need to reduce the amount of oil in the soap recipe to take into account the infusion oil. In this instance, you would weigh the oil for your recipe, then remove 2 tablespoons.

Soap colored with pink kaolin clay (top) and paprika (bottom).

You will replace these 2 tablespoons by adding the oil that has been colored with annatto seed into the soap at trace.

Another way to infuse botanicals is to put them with a liquid oil in a sealed jar and allow it to steep at room temperature for several weeks or until the desired color is reached. Strain the solids and use 2 tablespoons per batch of soap at trace. Again, remember to reduce the oil in the recipe by 2 tablespoons.

Essential Oils and Natural Fragrance Oils

Essential oils are the concentrated oils extracted from plant leaves, flowers, and berries. Natural fragrance oils combine essential oils with other natural aromatic ingredients. (If not labeled "natural fragrance oil," a scented oil probably contains chemical ingredients.) Usually, fragrance oils are less expensive than essential oils.

Be sure you use only cosmetic-grade oils or those made specifically for soap making. As a general rule, use no more than 6 to 10 teaspoons per single batch of soap (4- to 5-pound finished brick). Fragrance and essential oils are available at craft stores, herb shops, and through online soap making suppliers.

Scent Categories of Popular Essential and Natural Fragrance Oils

Floral
Geranium
Lavender
Lilac
Lily of the Valley
Rose

Citrus
Grapefruit
Lemon
Lemongrass
Lime
Orange

Aromatherapy
Lavender
Peppermint
Spearmint
Ylang Ylang

Woodsy/Earthy
Atlas Cedarwood
Balsam
Bay Laurel
Juniper Berry
Musk
Oak Moss
Patchouli
Sandlewood

Seasonal
Balsam
Bay Laurel
Peppermint
Pine
Spruce

Experiment with Fragrance

Perfumes and colognes are a complex blend of oils and other ingredients. Scent is very subjective, so a fragrance you love may not please everyone.

Depending on the oils you use, your soap can smell citrusy, musky, flowery, spicy, or woodsy. When several oils are combined, some will evaporate faster, and the remaining oils will take over. You may want to play it safe at first by using just one scented oil or following a proven winner recipe. Later, you can have some fun experimenting by using multiple scented oils in your recipes.

Soap scent is strongest when soap is freshly made and diminishes over time.

Chapter 2

How to Make Cold Process Soap

BASIC THREE-OIL SOAP RECIPE

Single batch to fill a 4- to 5-pound mold

Measure the following ingredients by weight:

  14 ounces palm oil

  18 ounces olive oil

  16 ounces coconut oil

  7.10 ounces sodium hydroxide

  17.5 ounces distilled water

Measure the following ingredients by volume:

  6 teaspoons fragrance or essential oils (You may
    combine multiple fragrance oils, but the total
    amount should be 6 to 10 teaspoons)

  1/2 cup ground oats or other additive

Superfatting Soap Recipes

All of the recipes in this book have been "superfatted." Superfatting leaves un-saponified oils in the final soap. Unsaponified oils have not formed compounds with the other soap making components. They remain in their original form in the final bar as emollient ingredients.

Superfatting is beneficial in several ways. It is a safety measure that protects you from having too much sodium hydroxide in the soap, which can be harsh on skin. This becomes especially important when you concoct your own soap recipes using the saponification chart on page 81. Superfatting also produces a milder soap that's smooth and creamy.

To superfat a soap recipe, the amount of sodium hydroxide used in a perfectly calculated recipe is reduced, or "discounted," by a certain percentage. Recipes in this book are discounted by 5 percent. This means that the correct amount of sodium hydroxide required for complete saponification is reduced by 5 percent.

The negative aspect of superfatting is that the soap may not last as long. Five percent–superfatted soaps should last at least six months (and typically longer) before the oils start becoming rancid.

You may add a natural preservative such as grapefruit seed extract to extend the life of superfatted soaps. Use about 6 to 7 grams per 4- to 5-pound batch of soap that is 5 percent discounted. Essential oils, herbal infusions, and dried herbs may also help preserve superfatted soap.

Always remember to "tare" your scale each time you weigh an ingredient. To do so, place the empty container on the scale and set the counter to zero. This allows you to easily weigh only the ingredient, not the container, too.

1 **Get ready.** Start by assembling all of your equipment and ingredients so that they are within arm's reach.

2 **Prepare the mold.** If you are using a wood mold, you must first line it with freezer paper or parchment paper with the shiny side up,
Cut one sheet to fit the long sides and one sheet to fit the short sides of the mold.

Use your fingers to crease the paper along the edges.

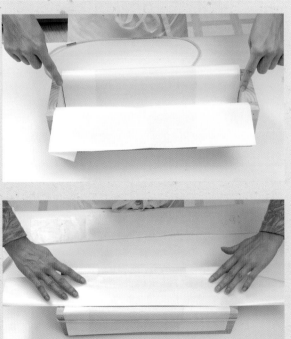

Secure the lining to the mold with a mold strap, rubber band, or large binder clips.

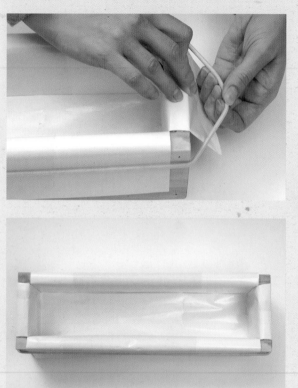

3 **Prepare the oats.** Measure out ½ cup of oats. Use traditional rolled oats or plain oatmeal rather than the instant type. Grind the oats into a finer consistency with a mortar and pestle or an electric coffee grinder

With a mortar and pestle, you use a twisting motion to press the oats between the pestle and the sides of the mortar until you reach the desired flake size. You'll achieve better results if you grind a little at a time.

Using a coffee grinder is faster—but because of that, you risk grinding your oats (or other botanicals) into a finer powder than you are aiming for.

Control the grind by placing a small portion of the oats in the grinder and pulsing for a second or two. Check the results and pulse again if necessary until the oats are a consistent size.

Place the ground oats in a bowl and set aside.

4 **Mix the sodium hydroxide and water.** Place your scale on a protected surface. With your safety gear on, place your empty container on the scale and tare the scale. Pour 17.5 ounces of distilled water into your container. Set this aside.

Place another empty (non-aluminum) container on the scale and tare the scale again. Carefully pour 7.1 ounces of sodium hydroxide into the container. Remove the container from the scale.

5 **Mix the sodium hydroxide and water.** Slowly and carefully pour the sodium hydroxide into the water. (Never pour water into lye.) Use a non-aluminum spoon or spatula to stir the solution until the sodium hydroxide is completely dissolved. This will take a couple of minutes.

As you stir, the solution will become quite hot. Set the stirred solution aside in a safe place to cool to about 100 degrees Fahrenheit.

6 **Prepare the oils.** While the sodium hydroxide solution is cooling, you can prepare the oils. Place your empty container on the scale. Tare your scale and pour 18 ounces of olive oil into a container.

Incorporating solid oils or butters into your mixture requires an additional step. You must first liquefy the oil or butter prior to adding the sodium hydroxide mixture.

There are two ways of doing this:

Method 1: Stove Top

Select a pot that's large enough to hold both solid oils. Place it on your scale and tare the scale.

Add 14 ounces of palm oil to the pot.

Place the pot with the palm oil on the scale and tare the scale again.

Add 16 ounces of solid coconut oil right on top of the palm oil.

Place the pot on the stove on medium-high heat. Never leave oil on a hot burner unattended. Oils can overheat, smoke, and catch fire if overheated.

Stir occasionally until the solid oils are almost completely liquefied. Leaving a few small solid pieces will ensure that you do not overheat the oil. Remove the pot from the stove and turn off the burner. Stir the oils until all of the small pieces are dissolved.

Method 2: Microwave

Place the correct amount of solid oils in a microwave-safe bowl. (If you are using multiple kinds of oil, you will want to melt them separately because different oils melt at different temperatures.)

Microwave on medium-high for a short 20- to 30-second burst. Stir the oil. Microwave again for another 20 to 30 seconds, and stir again. Continue in this way until the solid oil is completely liquefied.

7 Combine all oils. Pour the olive oil and liquefied palm and coconut oils into the same non-aluminum pot. Blend them by gently stirring.

8 **Take temperature readings.** The ideal time to blend the two mixtures is when the sodium hydroxide/water solution is at 100 degrees F and the temperature of the oils is at 100 degree F, plus or minus 10 degrees.

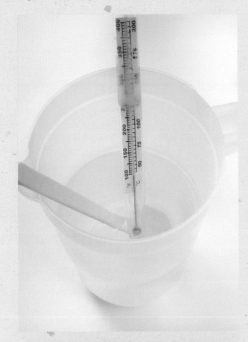

9 **Combine sodium hydroxide/water solution and oils.** Wearing your safety gear, carefully pour the sodium hydroxide solution into the blended oils. Use a non-aluminum stirrer to loosely combine all of the ingredients.

10 **Stir until trace is reached.** Using the same utensil or the stick blender, stir the mixture as you would if preparing cake batter.

The trickiest part of this process for new soap-makers is determining when proper "trace" is reached.

Trace is the point at which most of the chemical reaction—"saponification"—has taken place. The amount of time it takes to reach the trace stage depends on the oils you use and the temperature of the mixture.

As you stir, you will see the soap mixture turn from a clear golden color to an opaque light beige or yellow. Initially, when you lift your stick blender or spoon out of the mix, the liquid will stream off quickly. As you continue stirring, the liquid will drip off the blender more slowly.

Once a small amount of soap drizzled across the surface of the mixture leaves a pattern on the surface, you have reached light trace.

11 **Add essential oil or fragrance oils.** Add 6 teaspoons of fragrance or essential oil per single batch (or up to 10 teaspoons if you want a strongly scented bar). You may add a single scent or multiple scents, as long as you keep the amount between 6 to 10 teaspoons per single batch.

Mix in the fragrance oils loosely with a whisk and then switch back to your stirrer or stick blender. Blend the oils in for about 15 seconds with a stick blender; 30 seconds if stirring by hand. Do not overstir or your mixture will become too thick.

It's a good idea to make notes if you are creating your own recipes. That way, you'll know what worked and what did not after the soap is finished. You cannot adequately evaluate the scent until the soap is fully saponified.

12 **Add ground oats.** Pour ½ cup of ground oats into the mixture. Use a whisk or spoon to incorporate the oats evenly throughout the mixture.

When to Add Botanical Additives

Fragrance oils, essential oils, and most botanical additives should usually be added at light trace. Keep in mind that some additives, such as honey, oats, and clays, will thicken the oil mixture substantially as soon as they are added.

The exceptions to adding ingredients at light trace are if you want a layered soap, if you plan to embed objects in the soap, or if you want small, light additives (such as seeds, grains, or lavender flower buds) to be uniformly suspended in the soap. These are added when the mixture reaches what is called "heavy trace."

To reach heavy trace, you would continue stirring the mixture for a minute or two until it becomes very thick, like brownie batter, and much more difficult to stir with a spoon. At heavy trace, a spoonful of oil mixture will resist falling off the spoon for several seconds.

13 **Fill the mold.** Pour the mixture into your mold. This lined, wood soapmaker's mold will make a standard single-batch soap brick that measures 12¾ by 3¼ by 3¼ inches.

Lightly tap the mold onto the counter to remove air bubbles. Place a sheet of plastic wrap over the soap and press it down lightly to remove any surface bubbles.

If you are using plastic storage containers or other lined molds, you can fill them up close to the rim. A standard bar of soap is about 3 to 3½ inches tall.

14 **Put the soap to bed.** Place a lid over your mold and fold a towel over the mold on all sides. Put filled molds in a place where they will remain undisturbed. Then add an additional towel on top.

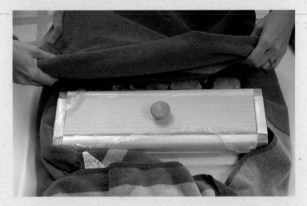

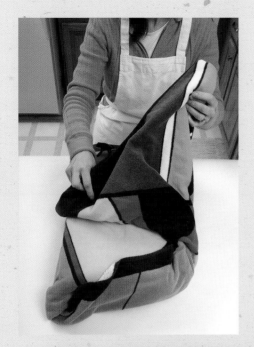

At this point, most of soap is saponified; however, the chemical reaction will not be totally complete for another 24 hours.

Keeping the soap at an evenly warm temperature is essential to finishing the saponification process. Don't move the molds during this period. Even a little motion can change the uniform shape of the finished brick.

15 **Do the dishes.** Because the saponification process is not one hundred percent complete at this point, leave your gloves on for the cleanup.

Use paper towels to scrape off the bulk of the soap. Place paper towels in a trash bag and place the bag where pets or children can't get into it.

A squirt of dishwashing liquid will help remove the small bits of handmade soap from your equipment.

16 **Unmold soap.** After a full 24 hours has passed, your soap brick is ready to be unmolded. If you don't have time to unmold it right away, you can wait up to a week to do so. After a week, however, the soap will harden and become more difficult to slice.

Remove the lid and carefully peel off the plastic wrap. The lining paper serves as a useful handle to remove the soap brick from the mold.

If you are using plastic containers, pull the mold away from the brick on both long sides at once, then on both short sides.

Peel off the lining paper.

17 **Cut brick into bars.** You can use a large kitchen knife to cut bricks into bars; however, a pastry cutter/chopper is easier on the hands. Usually the ends of the molds are uneven, so take off a narrow slice to create a clean face.

Then, measure about 1 inch from the end and push the cutter vertically into the soap.

A serrated pastry cutter creates interesting sides.

18 **Finish the Edges.** Your soap will have a more finished appearance if you use a vegetable peeler to shave off the edges and any uneven parts. Save these scraps in a sealed plastic container. You can use them later to make confetti soap (see page 47) or soap balls (see page 46).

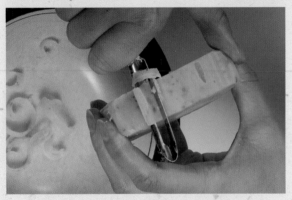

19 **Cure the bars.** The soap *can* be used right away, but the bars will disintegrate faster in water and won't be as gentle on the skin. To obtain the hardest, mildest bars, cold process soap should be cured for about a month before it is used. Cure bars by placing them on edge on a cookie sheet or tray lined with waxed paper, parchment paper, or freezer paper (shiny side up). Place the tray in a cool, dry location out of direct sun.

How to achieve an evenly colored bar

Some additives, like the essential oils and oats used in this recipe, can be added directly to the main batch of soap. Additives used to color soap—clays, herbs, roots, cocoa powder, or oxide powder—are best mixed with a small quantity of the soap mixture prior to being added to the main batch. Otherwise you may have splotches of darker color within your soap bar.

1 Measure the amount of the additive you need into a small bowl.

2 Pour about 2 cups of the soap mixture (a light trace) on top and whisk together until thoroughly incoporated. With clay, be sure to stir until no lumps remain.

3 Make adjustments, if needed. If you want a stronger color, now is the time to add more colorant.

4 Pour the additive mixture back into the main soap mixture.

5 Use a wire whisk or spoon to thoroughly combine the additive into the main mixture.

20 **Store the soap.** Soap should not be stacked for storage. Place the bars on edge with space between in a plastic storage box or a shoe box. Keep the box in a cool, dark place until needed.

Using a soap cutter

A professional soap slicer makes the job a breeze. A wood "stop" is placed at the desired thickness mark. The soap brick is pushed forward against the stop. The knife or pastry cutter is inserted into a cutting groove, which ensures that the cut will be vertical. This tool is well worth the investment if you plan on making soap in bulk.

BASIC SOAP RECIPES

Here are several recipes you may want to try to practice weighing your ingredients and determining the point at which you reach trace. They all use inexpensive oils that you may already have in your pantry. Make notes for future reference on the special properties of each bar, such as its hardness, amount of lather created, how it feels on the skin, and its conditioning and moisturizing properties. This will help you learn to achieve the effects you want in your own custom soaps. Each of these recipes makes a 4-pound batch of soap.

Basic Soap Recipe #1

Olive Oil	12 ounces
Castor Oil	8 ounces
Peanut Oil	12 ounces
Shortening (Crisco)	16 ounces
Water	17.5 ounces
Sodium Hydroxide	6.19 ounces (5% superfat)
Essential or Fragrance Oils (if desired)	6 teaspoons

Basic Soap Recipe #2

Olive Oil	12 ounces
Coconut Oil	12 ounces
Canola Oil	12 ounces
Shortening (Crisco)	12 ounces
Water	17.5 ounces
Sodium Hydroxide	6.72 ounces (5% superfat)
Essential or Fragrance Oils (if desired)	6 teaspoons

Basic Soap Recipe #3

Olive Oil	16 ounces
Coconut Oil	16 ounces
Safflower Oil	16 ounces
Water	17.5 ounces
Sodium Hydroxide	7.04 ounces (5% superfat)
Essential or Fragrance Oils (if desired)	6 teaspoons

Chapter 3

Fun & Decorative Natural Soaps

Once you've mastered the basic bar, it's time to get creative with color and shape! By combining two different mixtures of soap, you can make bars with layers and swirls of different colors. Soap chunks and shavings can be recycled to make eye-catching nugget and confetti soaps. Molds in all shapes and sizes produce soaps that are ideal for seasonal use and gift giving. The cookie cutter, which is relegated to the cupboard for most of the year, takes on a new purpose. Grab your gear, assemble your supplies, and get ready to have some fun.

CUTOUT SHAPES

Repurpose that cookie cutter collection by using the cutters to make decorative soaps. Unmolding the soaps can be a bit tricky for molds that have deep indentations or curves, but otherwise, the process is easy.

If you don't have a special wood mold made for this purpose, a lined jelly roll pan works well. Any cold process soap recipe may be used, with additives and fragrance oils of your choice. Wash your cutters after you're done, and they'll be ready to make cookies again.

1 **Make the soap recipe.** Put on all safety gear. In separate containers, weigh distilled water and sodium hydroxide. Carefully combine sodium hydroxide and water and set aside.

In separate bowls, weigh olive, coconut, and palm oils. Melt the coconut and palm oils, and combine all the oils into the same pot. When the sodium hydroxide/water solution and the oils reach about 100 degrees, combine them. Stir until light trace is reached.

Fragrance oils, colorants, and other botanicals may be added at this point; stir the soap until they are incorporated throughout.

2 **Pour soap into the mold.** Pour the mixture into your prepared mold to the same depth as or slightly lower than the height of the cookie cutters you are using.

Tilt the mold to distribute the soap mixture evenly and tap it on the counter several times to release any trapped air bubbles.

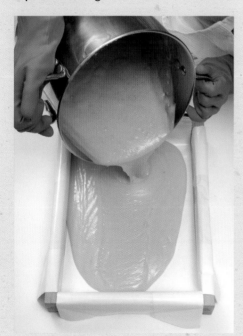

Cutout shapes soap recipe

(4 pounds for 1-inch thick cutouts in a standard tray mold that measures 9 by 12 inches)

Olive Oil	16 ounces
Coconut Oil	14 ounces
Palm Oil	14 ounces
Sodium Hydroxide	6.49 ounces (5% superfat)
Distilled Water	16 ounces
Essential or Fragrance Oil	6 teaspoons
Additives (as desired)	1/2 cup

3 **Put the soap to bed.** Cover the soap with clear plastic wrap, gently pressing it to the soap surface.

Place a lid on the top and wrap the mold in several layers of towels. Place it in a warm place where it will be undisturbed. With gloves on, wash up your equipment.

4 **Unmold the soap.** Wait at least 24 hours before unmolding your soap. To make the job of cutting the soaps easier, it is best to unmold and cut within three or four days, while the soap is still on the soft side.

As with unmolding a soap brick, grasp the sides of the lining material, pull the soap from the mold, then remove the liner.

5 **Cut the soaps.** Place your cutter close to the edge of the soap slab.

With even pressure, push the mold into the soap. Use work gloves if necessary to protect your hands.

Once the cutter is embedded, stand the soap brick on edge and continue pushing the cutter until it breaks through the back of the soap brick.

Gently remove excess soap from the cutter edges until the soap pops out of the cutter.

You can continue making the same shape or switch to other shapes.

Place your shape on a lined tray to cure for about a month, then package it up, and it will be ready to use.

After you wash the cookie cutters thoroughly, they can be used for food preparation again.

USING THE SCRAPS

There are several ways to use up your hand-made soap scraps left over from the cookie cutter project.

Soap Balls

These are great for everyday use in the kitchen or bath. Hand-molded soap balls are best made within a couple of days after the soap is made, while the soap is still maleable. If you wait a week or more, it may be too hard to form into a ball.

Warm up a small soap scrap in one hand. Continue to add small pieces, squeezing them together.

Roll the soap between your palms to form a ball. Place it on your drying rack to cure for about a month before using.

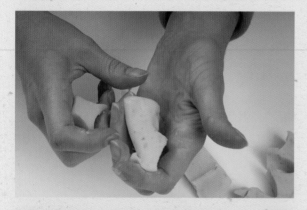

Nuggets and Confetti

Larger sections of scrap soap can be cut into uniform pieces to make nugget soap. Instructions for this soap start on page 53.

Or use a vegetable peeler to shred soap scraps. These odd-sized bits will be ideal for making confetti soap (page 56).

Keep nuggets and shredded pieces in plastic food storage containers until you're ready to use them.

Laundry Soap

Using cold process soap to do the laundry was a common practice before commercial soap products hit the market. To make your own soap powder, use the finest holes on a handheld shredder to grate one bar of homemade soap to a powder consistency. Thoroughly combine your finely grated soap bar with 1 cup washing soda and 1 cup borax.

Use ½ cup of this mixture per full load of laundry washed in a top-load machine. Use 2 tablespoons for a full load in a front-load machine. Homemade laundry soap is safe for HE (high-efficiency) machines, but you will want to follow the manufacturer's recommendations for the amount of soap to use. Should you find that the powder doesn't completely dissolve, liquefy the powdered soap by mixing it with a cup or two of hot water before adding it to the machine.

Rebatching

Soap scraps can be cut into similar-sized pieces, combined, and rebatched. Rebatching works best with soaps that include milk as a base. Soaps that are heavy in olive oil are the most difficult to rebatch. The key is to melt the soap scraps on a low temperature until all of the scraps have liquefied. While it can take several hours for the soap to completely liquefy, you can remold soap at the gel stage (only partially liquefied). The result will be a less refined-looking soap that may have visible scraps and shreds throughout.

A slow cooker or double boiler works well for this process. Sprinkle a couple of tablespoons of water over the top of the scraps. As the soap is melting, stir it occasionally to break up the scraps. Do not use high heat for this process. Start with medium heat and lower the temperature if the soap begins to smoke. Never leave soap unattended as it can catch fire if it becomes too hot.

If the soap starts to dry out, sprinkle a tablespoon or two of water on the surface and stir. Once the soap is melted, you can add additional fragrance, essential oil, or botanical additives. The quantity of fragrance and additives will be a judgment call based on the amount of soap you are rebatching. Pour or spoon the remelted soaps into molds and allow the soap to harden for 24 hours. Unmold the soap and place it on a drying rack until it hardens fully. Because this soap has already been saponified, it is safe to use right away.

SWIRLED AND LAYERED SOAPS

Contrasting colors combine into exotic swirled patterns or can be stacked in layers. This process shows how to use one batch of soap to make swirled bars.

Another option would be to make two batches of soap, and use different additive and colorant combinations for each batch. Just remember that you'll need an extra pot so that you can divide the mixture and two brick molds (or enough plastic containers to hold the increased quantity of soap mixture).

Ingredients

One batch of cold process soap
6 to 10 teaspoons fragrance or essential oil
1 to 2 tablespoon pink kaolin clay
Wood brick mold or suitable container molds

1 **Make a basic soap recipe.** Use a recipe from page 39 and follow the instructions for making cold process soap.

When the mixture reaches light trace (see page 30), add 6 to 10 teaspoons of fragrance or essential oils, if you wish.

Stir in the oils using a wire whisk or spoon, then switch to a stick blender (or continue with the spoon) and mix thoroughly. This will only take about 10 seconds with a stick blender, or about a minute by hand.

2 **Prepare the colorant.** Measure 1 table-spoon of pink kaolin clay (or an appropriate amount of the additive of your choice) and place it in a measuring cup or bowl that holds 2 cups.

Add about 2 cups of soap mixture to the clay. Use a wire whisk to thoroughly mix the clay into the soap. Make sure no clay clumps remain. If you want the color to be more intense, now is the time to make adjustments. Keep in mind that clay tends to dry out the skin, so you don't want to use too much.

3 **Mix and layer.** Pour one half of the uncol-ored soap mixture into your mold. Tap the mold onto your work surface to release any air bubbles and to level out the top.

Pour half of the pink clay mixture evenly over the first layer.

Pour the other half of the uncolored soap mixture on top of the pink clay layer.

Top it off with the remaining pink soap.

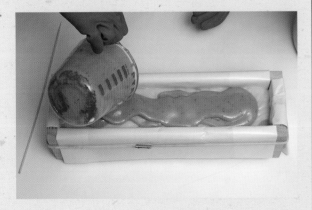

4 **Swirl the soap.** Stick a bamboo skewer or other thin stirrer into the soap mixture so that it reaches the bottom of the mold. Working from one end to the other, sweep the stick back and forth across the short sides of the mold.

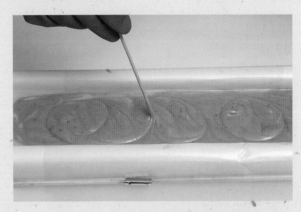

5 **Put your soap to bed.** Stretch clear plastic wrap over the soap surface and gently pat to remove high spots and air bubbles. Put a lid on top, wrap the mold in several layers of towels, and place it in a warm area on a level surface.

6 **Unmold the soap.** After 24 hours, unmold the soap.

Expect some surprises. Results can vary greatly depending on how thick your soap mixture was when you swirled it, the intensity of the colorant you used, and how energetically you stirred the colors together.

7 **Slice, cure, and finish.** The patterns are not quite revealed in the solid soap block. Once you slice the soap into bars, you'll see the interesting patterns that have formed.

Place the bars on a lined tray and put them in a dry, airy place to cure for at least a month.

Then use a vegetable peeler to neaten the edges, saving the scraps for later use.

Package the soaps individually or transfer them to a covered box or plastic storage container. Do not stack the soaps in storage.

Making two-layer soap

Making soap with two layers is similar to making swirled soap. Make a batch of basic soap. At light trace, incorporate fragrance and botanicals, if desired. This will thicken the mixture.

Pour half of the mixture into the mold. Add colorant to what remains in the bowl and mix until it is thoroughly incorporated. The mixture should be thick (heavy trace).

Then carefully and slowly pour the colored mixture on top of the layer of soap in the mold. This one-batch process will result in a blended efect rather than a perfectly straight line between the layers. (The two-batch process used for the black and tan soap on page 67 will result in a straight, precise line between the layers.)

Be careful not to tilt the mold or your layers are sure to shift, creating an uneven wave in the soap.

NUGGET SOAP

You can add dimension and interest to soap bars by combining chunks from a cured bar into a soap mixture of a contrasting color.

This enables you to use up scrap end slices from bricks you've made previously. Soap in any color and from any recipe may be used and is certain to produce unique results.

If you want more control over the results, you can make a brick of soap specifically to be used in nugget soap. That way, it will have a fragrance and color that will blend well with the main soap recipe you want to use.

1 **Prepare nuggets.** The first step in the process is to prepare your nuggets. Use a kitchen knife to cut the scraps or full bars into any shape and size you want—squares, rectangles, triangles, or free form.

2 **Make a basic soap recipe.** Add fragrance, colorant, and botonical additives, if desired, at light trace.

Stir until you reach heavy trace, when the mixture becomes very thick and swirls made by stirring remain on the surface for several seconds. Heavy trace is desirable when you want to suspend ingredients evenly throughout your soap bars.

3 **Add nuggets.** Slowly drop about 2 cups of nuggets into the soap batter and mix them in using a wire whisk or a spoon.

4 **Fill your mold.** Pour the mixture into your mold. At this point, the soap will be very thick, so use a spoon or spatula to get as much soap out of the pot as you can.

Level the surface of the soap and remove air bubbles by pressing the surface with the back of a spoon.

5 **Finish as you would a normal batch of soap.** As with swirled soap, you won't know what designs you will get until you slice the brick.

Confetti Soap

Confetti soap is a great way to use up the shavings obtained from trimming your soap bars. Make confetti soap the same way as nugget soap.

STAMPED SOAPS

Stamping offers a way to add decorative detail to plain soaps. As soap making has grown in popularity, so too has the variety of unique supplies that are available. Stamps designed just for making impressions on soap are among those specialty products. However, you can also use wood- or plastic-backed stamps designed for paper crafting. Even non-backed rubber stamps may be used.

The trick to obtaining a successful impression is to work on soap that is semicured. If it's too new and soft, the impression will be ragged and smear. If the soap is too hard, the stamp will crack the soap surrounding the stamp and ruin its appearance. Experience is the best teacher with this process, but soap that has been cured for 2 to 4 weeks seems to work best for most recipes.

Determine where you want to make your impression. Lightly place the stamp on the soap.

A rubber mallet is best because it reduces the likelihood of damaging the wood stamp handle, but a regular household hammer will also work.

Using light to medium pressure, tap the center of the stamp first, then tap each of the four corners. Go back to the center and tap again, and you're finished.

If you tap the hammer too hard, the soap could crack around the stamp edges. It's difficult, if not impossible, to reset a stamp and retap without getting a double impression. It's a good idea to practice stamping the extra slices you removed from the ends of your brick first.

If you're using an acrylic soap block stamp, don't hit it with a hammer—you could break it. Just press it firmly and evenly with the heel of your hand, front to back and left to right.

This rubber stamp does not have a wood or acrylic back but works just as well as a stamp made specifically for soap.

Position the stamp on the soap and use light to medium pressure to tap the entire surface of the stamp.

Tap several times to ensure that the entire design is embedded in the soap.

The stamp should peel off easily. After a quick rinse in water, the stamp will be ready to use for that next paper project.

DECORATIVE MOLDS

Here's your chance to break out of the rectangular brick mold! You can match any decor and coordinate your soap shapes with any holiday theme with plastic soap molds that are available in an array of shapes. You can also use molds made for candy making and baking. Plastic molds have become a mainstay for candy makers, and the recent addition to the culinary scene is the silicone rubber mold made for cupcakes and brownies. No lining material is needed for plastic or silicone molds. For the adventurous soul who wants something completely different from what is commercially available, you can buy liquid silicone from online suppliers and make your own soap molds.

1 **Fill the molds.** Start with a batch of soap made in your desired color and scent. Carefully spoon the soap mixture into each mold cavity, being careful not to overfill the mold.

2 **Level the surface.** Use the back of the spoon to level the top of the soap.

Gently tap the mold on the work surface to release any trapped air bubbles.

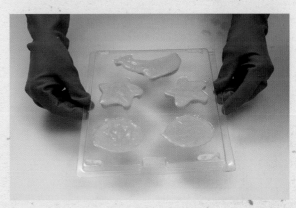

3 **Put the soap to bed.** Place a sheet of clear plastic wrap over the mold and gently pat onto the soap surfaces. Wrap your molds in two layers of towels and place them on a level surface in an area that will be undisturbed for 24 hours.

4 **Unmold the soap.** After 24 hours, you may unmold the soap; however, you may find that allowing the soap to set a few days longer will make the job easier.

To unmold, flip the mold upside down close to your work surface (in case some of the soaps pop out unexpectedly).

Apply gentle pressure on the center of the soap mold and the soap should come out into your hand.

5 **Tidy up the edges.** Use the vegetable peeler to even up rough edges. Save the scraps for later use.

If after a few tries the soap won't release, don't get rough. Simply place the mold into the freezer for 10 to 15 minutes and try again.

Correcting an Overfilled Mold

This mold used to make this dolphin was overfilled. Rather than trying to scrape the excess off the mold surface, which could create more of a mess, I waited to trim the soap after it had cured. You can use a sharp knife to cut away most of the excess soap, then use a vegetable peeler to clean up the edges.

Chapter 4

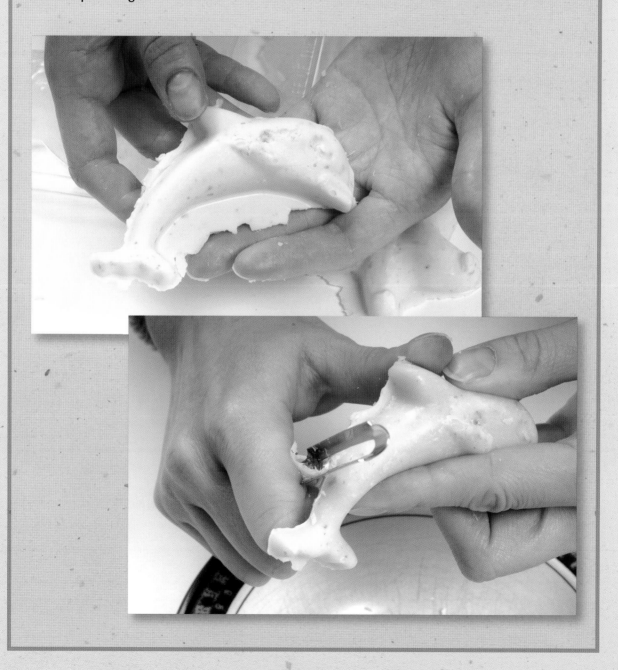

Special Soaps for Specific Purposes

As you now know, by blending various oils and using natural botanic ingredients, you can create a wide range of soaps: something smooth and creamy for facial use, a hard-working cleaning bar for hands, or an exfoliating, nutrient-rich bar for the bath or shower.

The soap recipes that follow use proven combinations to achieve specific goals. They will make welcome gifts or party favors and are not copyrighted, so you may make them to sell if you wish. Use these recipes as a foundation to craft your own soap creations, substituting additives and scents and changing the oils using the SAP values chart on page 81.

Enjoy the adventure.

ALL-NATURAL 'GENTLE' SOAP

Soft, smooth, and silky, this soap is great for bathing baby and for sensitive facial skin, too. You can't get more natural or simple than this one-oil soap. Olive oil–only soap has been made for millennia. It is often called "Castile" soap, referring to the Castile region of Spain where this soap was popularized by soap makers hundreds of years ago.

Recipe for one 4- to 5-pound brick

Olive Oil	48 ounces
Sodium Hydroxide	6.17 ounces (5% superfat)
Distilled Water	17.5 ounces

THE LAYERED LOOK IN BLACK AND TAN

Add mint, musk, or a woodsy oil such as sandalwood, and this soap is a natural addition to any man's sink or shower. Change the colors and oils and it takes on a feminine form. Add seeds or pumice to the tan layer to increase its exfoliation property. Or leave this mildly exfoliating recipe as is.

Recipe for one 4- to 5-pound brick

Charcoal Layer

Olive Oil	9 ounces
Coconut Oil	8 ounces
Palm Oil	7 ounces
Sodium Hydroxide	3.55 ounces (5% superfat)
Distilled Water	8.75 ounces
Activated Bamboo Charcoal	1 tablespoon
Essential or Fragrance Oil	3 teaspoons

Tan Layer

Olive Oil	5 ounces
Coconut Oil	7.5 ounces
Palm Oil	4 ounces
Jojoba Oil	3.5 ounces
Cocoa Butter	4 ounces
Sodium Hydroxide	3.3 ounces (5% superfat)
Distilled Water	8.75 ounces
Essential or Fragrance Oil	3 teaspoons
Cocoa Powder	1 tablespoon

Make the charcoal layer soap batch first and pour it into the prepared mold. Cover the top of the mold with towels, being careful that the towels do not touch the soap.

Then, prepare the tan layer (while you are doing this, the charcoal layer will thicken up, yielding a clean line between the layers). At heavy trace, carefully and slowly pour the tan layer on top of the charcoal layer.

WILD STRAWBERRY SOAP

Avocado oil, sweet almond oil, and shea butter blend wonderfully with the luxurious olive oil and coconut oil base to provide a bar that cleanses and moisturizes. The kaolin clay adds a soft, pink color. Change the scent and you'll have gifts for all of the holidays: lavender and rose for Valentine's Day, lily of the valley or lilac for Easter, and peppermint for Christmas.

Recipe for one 4- to 5-pound brick

Shea Butter	2 ounces
Olive Oil	10 ounces
Coconut Oil	15 ounces
Palm Oil	13 ounces
Avocado Oil	5 ounces
Sweet Almond Oil	3 ounces

Sodium Hydroxide	7.03 ounces (5% superfat)
Distilled Water	17.5 ounces
Strawberry Fragrance Oil	6 teaspoons
Pink Kaolin Clay	2–3 tablespoons

(more or less to achieve desired color)

Prepare the basic soap mixture. Measure the clay into a separate bowl or measuring cup. At light trace, pour about 2 cups of the soap mixture into the bowl containing the clay and fully incorporate it. Pour the 2 cups of clay mixture back into the soap and mix well. Add fragrance oils and stir to incorporate it throughout the soap mixture. Fill the mold.

GET UP AND GO! SOAP

A blend of lemon, lime, grapefruit, and orange will provide a citrus scent that will excite the senses. The aroma alone makes it ideal for use first thing in the morning and all day long in the kitchen. The castor oil produces increased lather and makes a bar that helps skin attract and retain moisture.

Recipe for one 4- to 5-pound brick

Olive Oil	16 ounces
Coconut Oil	16 ounces
Palm Oil	8 ounces
Castor Oil	8 ounces
Sodium Hydroxide	7.02 ounces (5% superfat)

Distilled Water	17.5 ounces
Essential or Fragrance Oils (citrus blends work well)	6 teaspoons
Turmeric	3 teaspoons
Paprika	1 teaspoon

Combine turmeric and paprika in a separate bowl or measuring cup. At light trace, add 2 cups of soap mixture into the spice mixture and mix well. Add fragrance and essential oils to the main pot of soap and mix well. Pour the spice/soap mixture into main pot of soap and mix well until heavy trace is achieved.

JAVA MINT SOAP

Mint is thought to revitalize and boost the spirits. This hand and body soap is great just about anywhere—the kitchen sink, the bath sink, or the shower. Peppermint essential oil provides the eye-opening fragrance, while coffee gives this bar a warm, rich color. Cinnamon provides exfoliating properties that will freshen dull skin. It is a great bar to remove those unwelcome odors, tough dirt, and oil.

Recipe for one 4- to 5-pound brick

Olive Oil	18 ounces
Coconut Oil	16 ounces
Palm Oil	14 ounces
Sodium Hydroxide	7.10 ounces (5% superfat)

Prepared Liquid Coffee	17.5 ounces
Peppermint Essential Oil	6 teaspoons
Cinnamon	2 teaspoons.
Coffee Grounds	2 tablespoons

Coffee should be made strong and dark using distilled water and then cooled to room temperature. Mix sodium hydroxide into prepared coffee and mix well. At light trace, add essential oil, cinnamon, and fresh coffee grounds and mix well until heavy trace is achieved. For hand soap, cut into 2-ounce (half) bars.

OATMEAL, MILK, AND HONEY

Nourished with buttermilk, this soap treats skin with extra care. Finely ground oats offer the slightest exfoliation to rid skin of dead skin cells, while beeswax lays down a protective layer. Jojoba oil helps nourish skin without blocking pores, and the honey acts as an emollient, drawing moisture, and adds natural scent and color to this soap.

Recipe for one 4- to 5-pound brick

Olive Oil	15 ounces
Coconut Oil	15 ounces
Palm Oil	13 ounces
Jojoba Oil	3.5 ounces
Beeswax	1.5 ounces
Sodium Hydroxide	6.73 ounces (5% superfat)

Distilled Water	12 ounces
Buttermilk	6.02 ounces
Ground Oats	½ cup
Honey	8–10 teaspoons

Melt the beeswax and other solid oils and then add to liquid oils. Add cold buttermilk to the distilled water. Add the sodium hydroxide slowly to the buttermilk/water combination. Add ground oats and honey at light trace.

BISCOTTI SOAP

This soap smells like you just stepped into an Italian bakery or coffee shop. Swirled cocoa powder contributes to the color and scent. It is enriched with olive oil to make skin feel clean and refreshed.

Recipe for one 4- to 5-pound brick

Olive Oil	18 ounces
Coconut Oil	16 ounces
Palm Oil	14 ounces
Sodium Hydroxide	7.10 ounces (5% superfat)
Distilled Water	17.5 ounces

Fragrance Oil (Biscotti or Similar)	6 teaspoons
Cocoa Powder	2–3 tablespoons

Measure cocoa powder into separate bowl or measuring cup. At light trace, combine two cups of soap into cocoa powder and mix well. Add fragrance oils to main pot of soap and mix well until medium trace is achieved. Pour soap into molds, only filling halfway. Pour half of cocoa powder mixture on top of soap in molds. Pour remaining soap from pot into molds. Pour remaining half of cocoa powder mixture on top of soap in molds. Using wooden skewer, gently swirl soap to combine.

GARDENER'S HAND SOAP

This soap is perfect for the hard-working hands of gardeners, mechanics, construction workers, or anyone who tackles messy projects. Jojoba oil and shea butter provide extra conditioning power. Ground herbs, oats, and cornmeal are used to exfoliate, leaving skin smooth and clean.

Recipe for one 4- to 5-pound brick

Shea Butter	4 ounces
Olive Oil	10 ounces
Coconut Oil	16 ounces
Palm Oil	13 ounces
Jojoba Oil	5 ounces
Sodium Hydroxide	6.76 ounces (5% superfat)

Distilled Water	17.5 ounces
Essential or Fragrance Oils (Berry Blend)	6 teaspoons
Ground Herbs	4 tablespoons
Ground Oats	¼ cup
Ground Cornmeal	¼ cup
Fragrance Oils of Choice	6–10 teaspoons

Add ground herbs, oats, cornmeal, and fragrance oils at light trace and mix until heavy trace is achieved.

GOAT MILK SOAP

This combination of oils produces a hard bar of soap that makes lots of lather. The goat milk makes the lather creamier and rapidly hydrates skin, and the olive oil provides lasting moisture. Adding the milk as a slurry helps prevent a burning aroma that can result from high heat.

Recipe for one 4- to 5-pound brick

Olive Oil	10 ounces
Coconut Oil	19 ounces
Palm Oil	19 ounces
Sodium Hydroxide	7.30 ounces (5% superfat)
Distilled Water	8.5 ounces
Goat Milk (Frozen/Slushy)	9 ounces
Essential or Fragrance Oil	6 teaspoons

Pour the goat milk into a freezer bag and freeze it until it clumps into chunks. Add this frozen slurry of goat milk into distilled water. Add sodium hydroxide slowly to the water/goat milk combination. Make sure the goat's milk does not reach a temperature above 120 degrees F. If necessary, add the sodium hydroxide in stages to keep the goat's milk at the proper temperature.

SKIN SOOTHER SOAP

This bar contains a secret ingredient: ground nettle leaf. This herb imparts a gorgeous green color and is believed to relieve itchy skin. The three oils combine to form a hard, moisturizing bar that lathers well. You may want to consider using ylang ylang oil (extracted from the flowers of an Asian tree). Aromatherapists find that this scent reduces anxiety, tension, and stress—a feel-good remedy for the body and the mind.

Recipe for one 4- to 5-pound brick

Olive Oil	18 ounces
Coconut Oil	16 ounces
Palm Oil	14 ounces
Sodium Hydroxide	7.10 ounces (5% superfat)
Distilled Water	17.5 ounces
Essential or Fragrance Oil (Fresh Floral Scent)	6 teaspoons
Ground Nettle Leaf	2–3 teaspoons

Measure nettle leaf into a separate bowl or measuring cup. At light trace, add about 2 cups of soap to the herb and mix well. Add fragrance and essential oils to the main pot of soap and mix well. Pour the herb mixture into main pot of soap and mix well until heavy trace is achieved.

ALL-NATURAL SHAMPOO BAR

Hair can become dry and dull when washed frequently with a commercial soap bar. Not so with this cold process shampoo bar. The combination ensures smooth, shiny results. It also serves as a hair conditioner and may be used as a body bar, as well.

Recipe for one 4- to 5-pound brick

Shea Butter	2 ounces
Olive Oil	5 ounces
Coconut Oil	14 ounces
Palm Oil	12 ounces
Castor Oil	8 ounces
Hemp Seed Butter	2 ounces
Avocado Oil	5 ounces
Sodium Hydroxide	6.91 ounces (5% superfat)
Distilled Water	17.5 ounces
Essential Oils (If Desired)	6 teaspoons

LUXURY BAR

Even the Ritz can't provide a better bar than this. Large amounts of jojoba oil and cocoa butter combine to form an extravagant, creamy, moisturizing treat for the skin. Splurge on the more expensive essential oils for this soap.

Recipe for one 4- to 5-pound brick

Olive Oil	10 ounces
Coconut Oil	15 ounces
Palm Oil	8 ounces
Jojoba Oil	7 ounces
Cocoa Butter	8 ounces
Sodium Hydroxide	6.6 ounces (5% superfat)
Distilled Water	17.5 ounces
Vanilla Essential Oil	6 teaspoons

If you want a white or light colored bar, substitute another essential oil for the vanilla fragrance, which gives the soap a brown tint. Note that the cocoa butter will impart a cocoa scent.

Chapter 5

Formulating Your Own Recipes

Cold process soap making melds art and science. Soap makers use their creativity to put together just the right oils, botanical additives, and fragrances to produce a product with unique properties. Once you've mastered the basics of combining the basic soap recipes with additives, you may wish to move on to creating custom recipes using your own blend of oils. To do so, you need to understand the science behind cold process soap making.

The chemical reaction that occurs between the oils and the sodium hydroxide and water solution is called saponification. Soap can be made with any animal fat or vegetable oil. Each oil has a saponification value or "SAP" value. The SAP value is the amount of lye it takes to saponify one unit of oil.

The easiest way to develop your own soap recipe is to take an existing recipe and replace one or two of the oils listed in it. To do so, you must recalculate the amount of lye and water needed. The saponification charts provided on page 81 provide the factors you need to calculate oil, sodium hydroxide, and water amounts.

Determining Sodium Hydroxide Amounts

To determine the amount of sodium hydroxide needed for a recipe, multiply the amount of oil you are using (measured by weight in either English or metric units, but not by volume) by the SAP value for that particular oil. If you are using a combination of oils, multiply each oil by its SAP value and add all the amounts together to get the total amount of lye needed for saponification.

Example 1: If you are using 32 ounces of olive oil, multiply that amount by 0.135 (olive oil's SAP value) to get 4.32 ounces of sodium hydroxide needed.

.136 (olive oil SAP value)
x 32 ounces of olive oil by weight
_____
4.32 ounces of sodium hydroxide by weight

Example 2: If you are using 32 ounces of olive oil and 10 ounces of hazelnut oil, multiply 32 by 0.135 (olive oil's SAP), and 10 by 0.136 (hazelnut's SAP value) to get 4.32 and 1.26, which added together comes to 5.68 ounces of sodium hydroxide needed.

0.135 (olive oil SAP value)
x 32 ounces of olive oil by weight
_____
4.32 ounces of sodium hydroxide by weight

0.136 (hazelnut SAP value)
x 10 ounces of hazelnut oil by weight
_____
1.36 ounces of sodium hydroxide by weight

4.32 ounces of sodium hydroxide by weight
+ 1.36 ounces of sodium hydroxide by weight
_____
5.68 ounces of sodium hydroxide by weight

Superfatting

Until you are very familiar with soap making, it is highly recommended that you superfat your soap. When you "superfat" a recipe, you reduce the amount of sodium hydroxide in the recipe (referred to as "discounting"), ensuring that there is extra oil in the mixture and no lye is left in the final bar. This is mainly a safety factor, but it has an added bonus: Because of the extra oils which are left unsaponified, "superfatted" soap is often less harsh and more moisturizing than regular soap.

Reducing the sodium hydroxide by 5 to 10 percent is generally satisfactory. All the recipes offered in this book have a built-in superfat factor of 5 percent.

Keep in mind that the higher the percentage of oil—the more superfatted the recipe—the softer the soap will be. A softer soap is milder on the skin, but it will dissolve faster when used. You need to find a balance when creating a recipe so that the resulting soap is mild yet hard enough to be long lasting.

You might find that you prefer a soap superfatted at a different percentage. Careful record keeping as you make soap will allow you to adjust the amounts of sodium hydroxide, lye, oil, and water when you make subsequent batches.

To superfat your own recipes at 5 percent, you must reduce the amount of lye used in the recipe. This is most easily accomplished by multiplying the amount of lye needed by the complement of 5 percent—95 percent (.095). So, in Example 1, which calls for 4.32 ounces of sodium hydroxide, you superfat the recipe at 5 percent by multiplying 4.32 by 0.95 to get 4.10 ounces of sodium hydroxide:

4.32 ounces sodium hydroxide
x .95 discount factor

4.10 ounces of sodium hydroxide

Example 2 would require 5.4 (rounded up from 5.396) ounces of sodium hydroxide for a superfat percentage of 5 (5.68 x 0.95).

5.68 ounces of sodium hydroxide
x .95 discount factor

5.4 ounces of sodium hydroxide

Determining Water Amounts

The amount of water required for a particular batch of soap is directly related to the amount of sodium hydroxide. It is also directly related to the total weight of the fats and oils. The amount of water used should be between 30 and 38 percent of the total weight of the fats and oils..

To determine the amount of water needed for a recipe, multiply the amount of sodium hydroxide by 30 to 38 percent. All recipes in this book use 37 percent.

Example 1: 32 ounces of olive oil by weight x 37% = 11.84 ounces of water.

Example 2: 32 ounces of olive oil by weight + 10 ounces of hazelnut oil by weight = 42 ounces of oils.

42 ounces of oils by weight x 37% = 15.54 ounces of water.

As your soap dries, there will be some evaporation of water. The final batch, when cut into bars, will not have the same total weight it had before drying.

Saponification (SAP) value chart

Fat or Oil	SAP Value
Almond Oil	0.136
Apricot Kernel	0.137
Avocado Oil	0.133
Borage Oil	0.133
Canola Oil	0.132
Castor Oil	0.128
Cocoa Butter	0.137
Corn Oil	0.136
Evening Primrose Oil	0.136
Jojoba	0.069
Kukui Nut Oil	0.135
Lanolin	0.074
Lard	0.139
Macadamia Nut Oil	0.139
Neem Oil	0.137
Olive Oil	0.135
Palm Kernel Oil	0.177
Palm Oil	0.142
Peanut Oil	0.136
Rapeseed Oil	0.132
Safflower Oil	0.137
Sesame Oil	0.133
Shea Butter	0.129
Shortening (Crisco)	0.137
Soybean	0.136
Sunflower Seed Oil	0.136
Tallow, Beef	0.141
Walnut Oil	0.135
Wheat Germ Oil	0.132

Testing the pH of Your Soap

Superfatting soap helps ensure that all of the sodium hydroxide in the soap has fully saponified and is no longer caustic. Any sodium hydroxide that remains in soap is called "free lye" and can burn the skin. If you are new to soap making or are trying out a new recipe, it's a good idea to do a pH test.

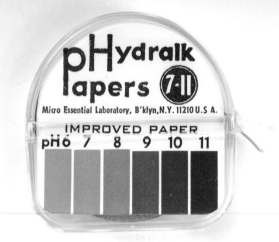

The pH is the measure of a solution's acidity or basicity. For example, water has a netural pH of about 7, a lemon is acidic with a pH of 2, and milk of magnesia is basic with a pH of 10. Lye is a very caustic base with a pH of 14. Cured soap should have a pH in the range of 8 to 10 (although a neutral pH of 7 or 7.5, or a high of 10.5, is acceptable).

Test kits for pH may be found at some hardware stores, at pet stores in the aquarium department, at swimming pool supply stores, and of course, online.

A pH test is easy to do:

1 Place a generous drop or two of tap water onto the soap surface.

2 Place the end of the test strip in the water for the amount of time recommended in the instructions. Usually, this tales only a few seconds.

3 Match the color of your strip with the color on the chart that accompanies the kit. The soap illustrated here has a pH of 8.

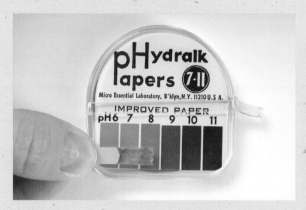

While the results may not be super scientifically accurate, a home pH test will give you a close enough range to have confidence in your soap.

Conclusion

In this era of mass-produced, chemical-laden household goods, home-made soap is a natural alternative that is better for our skin and the environment. The many easily attainable and affordable ingredients you can use transform soap making from drudgery to a pleasant experience that involves a large measure of creative input. Here's hoping that you find the soap making process to be fun and rewarding, and that you will continue on to produce many batches of luxurious, aromatic soaps using your own unique recipes. Happy natural soap making to you in all the days ahead!